WHEN YOUR PARENTS DIVORCE

CHRISTIAN CARE BOOKS

Wayne E. Oates, Editor

WHEN
YOUR PARENTS DIVORCE

by

William V. Arnold

THE WESTMINSTER PRESS
Philadelphia

Book Design by Dorothy Alden Smith

Published by The Westminster Press ®
Philadelphia, Pennsylvania

PRINTED IN THE UNITED STATES OF AMERICA
9 8 7 6 5 4 3 2

Library of Congress Cataloging in Publication Data

Arnold, William V   1941–
    When your parents divorce.

    (Christian care books)
    Bibliography: p.
    1. Divorce—United States. 2. Children of
divorced parents—United States. 3. Emotions.
I. Title. II. Series.
HQ834.A8   301.42'84   79-20055
ISBN 0-664-24294-4

To my wife and daughter
Kathy and Allison

Contents

Continued

Preface

A book addressed to teen-age and young adult children of divorced parents must be more than a simple review of the literature on the subject. It requires cases and comments and insight from those who have lived through the experience. It is not enough to sit in an office and remember the many persons with such experience who had talked with me in the past. Through correspondence and conversation and consultation with older children of divorced parents I have been helped to focus the concerns that needed to be addressed. Even more importantly, what I have written has been shaped, informed, and improved by their responses and criticism.

While I take responsibility for what is written, I received valuable assistance along the way. Thus, there are many persons to be thanked, some of whom would prefer that their names not be printed. Thanks can be expressed directly to Olivia Brown and Marty Johnson for their willingness to correspond with me from the position of adults reflecting back. Thanks, too, to the young people in Newport News who met with their minister, Bob DeWester, to discuss their experiences and to respond to the book as it was being written. They are: Mary Beth and Tommy Myles, Mark Myer, Anne Jennings, and Ann Davis. Linda Johnson, another young person whose parents are divorced, was kind enough to read the book in almost final form and make suggestions. All these people have made sure that these pages were more alive and realistic than an academic study of the subject would have been.

Betty Hopkins has shown good humor, dedication of spirit, and intense interest as she has typed the manuscript. For that I am deeply grateful.

W.V.A.

Introduction

"What can a book tell me about experiencing the divorce of my parents? After all, if I've been through it, there are a good many things I could tell you. Right?"

"I need someone or something to help me make sense out of this mess we have all gone through—parents, myself, brothers and sisters. It was a mess, is a mess, and looks like it's going to continue to be a mess!"

"Thank goodness it's over! The fights, the silences. The long, unexplained absences. It's a relief. That's what the divorce of my parents is—a real relief!"

All those expressions, and more, are ones that I have had to bear in mind in writing this book. There is much variety in them, as you can readily see. At the same time, there is a lot of commonality. I hope to provide some perspectives that will help in your pilgrimage as the son or daughter of divorced parents.

First, I would like to introduce myself. My name is Bill Arnold. I am a thirty-seven-year-old Presbyterian minister who, at this time, is teaching pastoral counseling at a seminary in Richmond, Virginia. In my experience as a hospital chaplain and later as the minister of pastoral care at a large church in Louisville, Kentucky, my interest has focused on the experience of divorce. I organized a group for divorced persons in that church. One of the outcomes of the group was a book for divorced persons and for persons considering divorce. It wasn't just my own work. Rather, it was authored by me and three members of the group.

I was delighted to be asked by the editor of this series to address a book to those whose parents have divorced. Much has been written to and about "children" of divorce, meaning those under the age of eleven or twelve. But for those of you who are teen-agers, there is much less. For those of you who are young adults, virtually nothing has been written.

What are the reasons for that? I have some thoughts about it and plan to share them with you, but the point here is to say that this book is consciously and pointedly prepared for you, the older adolescent or young adult whose parents have divorced, whether recently or some time ago. Regardless of when divorce occurred, you know from your experience and I know from the many folks to whom I have listened, that it leaves an imprint. All too often it's an imprint that people don't seem to want to hear about. The book, then, is for you, the sons and daughters of divorce.

Where to begin? Divorce has effects on our feelings, our thoughts, our present actions, and our future commitments. That is the order in which I will try to deal with your issues. Because adjustment to a divorce is a process, some of these areas will be more alive for you than others, but stick with me, all the way through, please. Understanding where you've been is as important as knowing where you are and where you're going.

In Part I, the section on feelings, there will be several areas. One is anger—the sense of outrage or bitterness you may feel about the divorce of your parents. You may be more aware of a sense of sadness, or grief, over the loss of the parental relationship. The anger or the sadness may be accompanied by feelings of guilt, abandonment, or blame. Others of you may feel more relief, or even joy, that the marriage has ended so that the pain will be over. Most of us, being human, don't feel a pure emotion. Instead, often we have a bewildering mix of all these and more. Let's sort out some of these feelings to help you gain a grip on where you are in this array.

In Part II, we'll tackle thoughts. There is a difference, you know, between feelings and thoughts. Our culture tends to confuse feeling and thinking, as if they were the same thing. To say, "I feel that divorce is wrong," is not a feeling. It's a thought, a judgment, an attempt to justify a feeling of pain or outrage at the effects of a divorce. We, in fact, have both feelings and thoughts about many experiences, and it is best to be conscious of the differences lest they contaminate each other. Thoughts about divorce are important. How do you get some distance and reflect on what has happened? What do you *think* about the way divorce is regarded religiously? What do you *think* the impact of your parents' divorce has been on you? Those are the concerns of this second section.

In Part III, I will lend some help in assessing behavior, or response, to your thoughts and feelings. What are you *doing* to and for yourself? to and for your parents? to and for your friends? Are they things that are consistent and things you want to be doing? My concern will then turn to your commitments, or long-range plans. What is your commitment to marriage now, after you have experienced the divorce of your parents? What changes of commitment have come about? Are there nagging inconsistencies in your commitments because of what has happened? How do they affect your relationships, your vocation, your sense of trust in people, in God? Where to from here?

I hope you're with me.

PART
I
FEELINGS

1. Sometimes Mad

A twenty-three-year-old woman came to tell me that she had just learned her parents were separating and would probably divorce. Her mother had called and wanted her to come home. "I'm not going," she said, "because I might say something I shouldn't. I'm mad!"

Anger—a feeling or emotion that is commonly felt when a divorce is announced and long after. Unfortunately, it's complicated by the reaction of many that it should not be felt, or at least not expressed. Nevertheless, it's there, in one way or another, for everyone whose parents have divorced. Why?

Generally speaking, anger is our internal response to an experience of having been blocked from having or getting something we want. And usually the anger is intensified if there is the perception that we have been blocked unjustly or when we didn't deserve it. That's where anger comes in for you.

The fact of the matter is *you didn't deserve to have your parents divorce* and thus deprive you of a normal, primary experience of family life. You have been cheated by their failure to carry through with their relationship in a healthy way. And the normal emotional response to that is anger.

"Now hold on," you may say. "Isn't that a little harsh? After all, they married with good intentions; they tried hard; they didn't want this to happen; there wasn't any other choice."

All of that is true. That is an accurate, logical description of their experience, and they certainly have been through much pain in arriving at such a decision. At the same time, you will not have a primary experience of family life because of their inability. And thus, through no fault of your own, you have been blocked from a very important experience in your life.

I would like to help you understand some of the experiences you will have. Let me hasten to add that it is not my intent to launch you into some exaggerated "getting all the anger out" that is commonly associated with distorted forms of encounter experiences. I do want you to be able to see and acknowledge this fact of divorce without distortion. And there are many distortions to which you may be tempted to resort.

1. One major distortion that you may experience is *self-blame*, the assuming of responsibility for the fracture in your parents' marriage. It's easy for a person to slip into such self-blame without realizing it. The most common way is through searching for a reason, an explanation for what happened. Children around the ages of five to seven do this most graphically. All too often they assume that since, on occasion, they wished Mom or Dad would go away, now it has really happened. And so they experience guilt.

We adults are more subtle and elusive in our ways of blaming ourselves. Perhaps you are aware that your birth was not planned. Maybe you were born at a time when an extra person created extra pressure on the marriage. Since you were around, the pressure was created; *therefore,* your existence *caused* the divorce. The next emotional (not logical) step is to think, If it weren't for me, they wouldn't have divorced. Don't forget that we are talking about distortion of anger. Blaming yourself is a way to avoid admitting that you are angry, to avoid voicing the resentment at not having the benefit of a lasting relationship with two adults who form the basis for your home. It's frightening to think of attacking two persons who are already down. Better, we think in our discomfort, to attack ourselves. But that is a heavy price to pay. An important part of your own future adjustment is to acknowledge to yourself (not necessarily to your parents) that *they* have cost you something. To take the blame on yourself is to leave you to carry a burden that is not yours. To see the picture realistically, and thus allow yourself to experience the reality of your loss, frees you to cope with the situation in a responsible and healthy manner.

The woman to whom I referred at the beginning of this chapter waited a month to go to visit her parents. During that time she voiced to me on several occasions her anger at having to feel that her home was gone, knowing that visits with her mother and father would be separate, that her future child would not know the joy of visiting grandparents together. Having acknowledged her losses and her changed future, she was then able to go for the visit in a manner that was responsible to herself and to her parents. She was able to do that in part because of admitting her anger to herself and to another. It was "speakable" and thus less likely to get out of control.

2. A second distortion that may occur over anger is *exaggerated hostility*. I make a distinction between anger and hostility. Anger is the internal feeling. Hostility is an external expression of the anger. You may be angry and appear very cool to those around you. If you are hostile, however, there is no doubt in others' minds that you are angry. Some people appear hostile in their manner even though they are not experiencing anger at the time.

Exaggerated hostility appears in various forms: bitterness, temper tantrum, rage, incessant accusations, etc. There is nothing very subtle about any of its expressions: the seventeen-year-old son, living with his divorced mother, who consistently refuses to come home at the agreed time, saying, "You can't make me now that you don't have Dad around anymore"; the thirteen-year-old who suddenly bursts into rages, screaming, throwing things, and generally appearing out of control. Perhaps you have found yourself moving through periods, sometimes lasting weeks, of bursting out with vicious and hurting remarks, even surprising yourself. Even if you're no longer living at home, there may be a sudden attack about all the extra problems your mother and father have caused because of their separation. The hostility may be more indirect than that—repeated cynical comments made about marriage in the presence of parents or friends, sudden open distrust and dislike of men or women, fervent interest in exposing the ways in which persons of one sex use and abuse those of the opposite sex.

Care must be taken here to point out that some of these interests may have positive benefits. The criterion for evaluation is the *extreme* to which they may be carried. The exaggerated nature of the responses may well mean that you are *stuck* in the emotional process of coping with this experience. It means that the anger has become a controlling pattern in your life, disabling your ability to find ways of living that do not keep a preoccupying focus on the divorce and its consequences for you.

3. A twenty-year-old college student illustrates a third type of distortion that can occur around anger. I had heard of his parents' divorce, which was sudden and unexpected, and went to visit him. "It's O.K.," he smiled. "They are fine, and since I don't live at home anymore, it doesn't matter anyway. I'm not worrying about it and neither should you." *Apathy.* At least so it appeared. But far underneath that statement which appeared so "strong" and "in charge" was the message to his parents—"You don't matter to me." That is anger of an order that is frightening in many ways, because it reveals hurt so deep that the person will close off and see to it that no one will get close again.

Anger can be so powerful that it is frightening, and therefore we block it off altogether. Or we may have been taught in growing up that any expression of anger is wrong, so we stick a cork in the bottle. Unfortunately, we also stick a cork in our ability to grow and adjust. Apparent apathy or "nonfeeling" is often the expression of such repression. We may be so well trained in our ability to restrain feelings of anger that we really don't know when we are angry.

The price paid by my twenty-year-old friend is that in addition to the loss of the parental relationship which he would have liked to have, he has cut off *all* relationship. The cost is high enough without adding to it.

4. Anger is a feeling about which most of us experience discomfort. All too often the problem has been a lack of

discrimination between the feeling and the response to the feeling. We've been told, "Don't be angry," rather than, "Don't hit someone when you're angry." Thus, when we feel mad, a value judgment is there before we even get to know how to handle it. "If you're mad, you're bad." Not so!

When you're mad, you know the impact an experience has on you. And the anger helps you to deal more directly with a difficult experience. In the case of a parental divorce, anger is realistic and normal. What is unrealistic and abnormal is the tendency to blame yourself, to punish your parents and others interminably, or to ignore it.

Anger is a feeling. It's a vital clue to your health and vitality. Use it to help you face the reality of your loss. Here are some ways to do that:

a. If you haven't talked with anyone about what you will lose or what you have lost because of your parents' divorce, find a friend and ask if the person would be willing to listen.

b. After you've laid it out, and if you feel ready for some response, ask your friend whether you seem to be distorting in any of the ways I've discussed in this chapter. If you'd rather just have the friend listen and not get into evaluation, that's O.K. And tell your friend so.

c. If the anger seems to be pretty bothersome, try to learn more about it. Read *The Angry Book*, by Theodore Rubin, or *The Intimate Enemy*, by George Bach and Peter Wyden. These books will provide insight into how anger works for or against you.

d. If some real insight and new experience is coming out of this, keep up the conversation with your friend or spouse or minister.

e. If there seem to be some pretty intense issues arising, consider talking with a mental health professional. Your minister can suggest someone if he or she doesn't feel that he can work with you in this way.

Remember, we have been dealing with anger as a feeling. There will be thoughts about it to consider, evaluation to be made of your actions and ramifications for your long-term commitments as we move on.

2. Sometimes Sad

Sadness is a word that we use a lot. It can describe many different things. Usually something has been lost. It doesn't have to be a "thing." Perhaps some hopes and dreams haven't come true. Maybe a person you care about is going away for a short time, or even much longer. You may lose an idea about yourself, of who you thought you were or hoped to be. Sadness. That's one of the words that describe the feeling of having lost, whether it is a person, a dream, or a thing.

Sadness is a word that describes the feelings of most persons whose parents have divorced. It's not the only feeling, by any means. But it is an important one for many persons.

In fact, sad is a word that many persons use when they are grieving. Grief is the emotional process that we go through after a major loss. Usually we connect it with death. But the feelings are very similar after a divorce, not only with the sons and daughters of divorced parents. It is also a process through which a husband and wife must go after or during their divorce.

That process has stages that are helpful for you to know

25

about. I want to describe them now and ask you to read them slowly. After learning about each of them, stop reading for a moment and see if they are descriptive of what you have gone through. Remember that these stages aren't mechanical. You may experience some of them at the same time or even in a different order.

I. SHOCK

"I don't believe it!" That's the first stage, a period of both fearing that it's true and not believing that it's true. You may have lived in an atmosphere where loud arguments went on or stony silence took place. There may have been many fears that your mom and dad might split, but you usually didn't let yourself think about it for very long. Or there may have been times when you asked if they were going to get a divorce. Most children go through the stage of first learning about divorce when hearing about it at school. Then they wonder if it might happen in their own home.

But when the news comes, when someone actually sits down and says, "We're going to get a divorce," you just don't believe it. The disbelief can go on for various lengths of time. Maybe it will be only a few minutes, because things start to happen so fast that there is no way you can't believe it. It's happening right before your eyes. On the other hand, you may have a long period of time between the announcement of the decision and the actual occurrence of the moving and separating. That allows a longer period of time to think that it may not be true, that it is only a threat or a mistake. Then the stage of shock, of not believing it, may last much longer.

Of course, the shock will not be the same for everyone. For instance, if you were an infant when your parents divorced, you didn't have the decision announced to you. Growing up with one parent is the major memory you have. The shock is discovering it is different for other people.

But if you have had the pain of hearing the words, "We're getting a divorce," or have had it dawn suddenly on you that your parents are going to split, the first feeling is usually one of shock and disbelief.

Accompanying that first experience may have come a decision not to believe it, a determination to "see to it" that the divorce does not take place. Our emotions seem to pretend that something isn't true in the hope that refusing to acknowledge it may prevent it. That is another variation on shock and disbelief.

Another experience of shock is "forgetting," such as the young man who described getting home in the afternoon and expecting his father home at five o'clock. He regularly "forgot" that his father wouldn't be coming home anymore.

II. I'M AFRAID IT'S TRUE

The second stage of this process of grief is beginning to acknowledge that it is true. It comes in waves, not all at once. It's a period when you find yourself distracted from your schoolwork, thinking about something very different. Suddenly that feeling of sadness sweeps over you, often with no thoughts accompanying it. No respecter of time or place is that feeling. It may come in class, in the middle of a conversation, during a lazy afternoon, or while watching television or reading a book. "Wave" is the description of it that I know, because it simply rolls over you and then, after a short time, moves on.

As this stage progresses, you may find yourself staring off into space more so than usual. "Disconnecting" yourself from the rest of the world, finding it hard to concentrate, wishing you were somewhere else—all these are experiences of beginning to discover that it really is true. Your parents are going to get a divorce, or they have gotten a divorce.

It always has been amazing to me how miraculous it is that our psyches are able to absorb new and overpowering realities in our lives. You can see, just in examining these two stages, how something that is very devastating to us is not allowed to overpower us all at once. Instead, we absorb it a little at a time. That's why we talk about this sadness, or grief, as a process. It happens over a period of time, instead of all at once.

This second stage of the process is the most difficult one for me to describe to you because it is one of transition. You are moving from a firm stage of disbelief to the third one, in which there is no doubt that it is true.

III. It's True and It's Real

If you have been through it already, you know that this stage is the toughest one. You wish you could pretend it is not so, but you can't. You wish you could have some moments of relief, but they come very seldom. Sadness may not be a word that is powerful enough to describe this period. While the word and feeling we are talking about here is sadness, many other emotions crush in. Some are anger, guilt, loneliness, a sense of desertion.

One of the most powerful experiences is a sense of having no one to talk to who will understand. Or you may not want to talk to anyone even if you think the person would understand. If you have someone who is special to you, who will listen, then you are very fortunate. Especially is it fortunate if the person is there when you have the need, rather than that the person imposes on you when the time just may not be right for you. Many times your parents are the last ones you would want to talk to about these feelings. After all, they are having problems that have resulted in decisions that hurt very deeply—both themselves and you. Better to find someone else.

This is also a period when many questions run through your mind. Later on, they are thought out more carefully. Now, they are more forceful and are changing rapidly. One of the most powerful is the question of what home will be like now. One person said that the biggest issue that kept running through her mind during this phase was: Where will my home be? Will I have a home? Will I want to be at home?

Stop a moment now. Do these descriptions of feelings of grief thus far fit your own experience? What are the unique experiences and feelings you have had that help these stages become real for you? Is there someone you would like to talk to about them? Often a friend, a spouse (if you are now married), a minister, or some other person whom you trust can be very helpful during these periods in your life. Another person can't provide answers that will make the sadness go away. But knowing that someone cares helps.

IV. MEMORIES

After the intensity of the first three stages, there comes a period of remembering. It is much longer than the first three. And usually it is fairly well removed from the first time you *really knew* that the divorce was real. Your life is more predictable and your friends and activities have become more settled. Now is the time when you may *choose* to reconstruct what happened. There are times when you have questions that are less panicky, less intense, and ones that you can ask in less emotional ways.

Not only are there questions, but some evaluating begins to go on. You remember events from the time when both parents were at home, when things were very happy. And you miss those times. At other moments very painful or angering experiences come to mind, and you are relieved that you won't have to go through those anymore. Yet, what if? Perhaps that is the best descriptive phrase for this period. "What if?"

Later in this book I will be talking about some of these questions. They are occasions for very serious thought and meditation. Since this section of our discussion is concerned with feelings, however, I will postpone that discussion. If you have an interest in pursuing it right away, turn to any of Chapters 5 through 9. They deal with those concerns.

Take some time to do some remembering if it has been a while since your parents divorced. What kinds of memories come to mind? What regrets do you have? What kinds of satisfactions spring to your thinking? Are there any sources of sadness that you really haven't let yourself look at yet?

V. What Now?

The last of our stages of dealing with sadness, or grief, has to do with our actions. The divorce of parents and the breaking up of a family often leaves people paralyzed for a while. Certainly you may have kept up your activities, trying to look as though everything was O.K., but you know that you didn't really function at your best. Relationships in dating or in marriage may have continued, but often they stopped growing for a while. After all, your emotional energy was tied up with other things. If you were still in school, you *may* have continued to do your homework, but you found that it was difficult to concentrate on it or in class.

When you feel yourself picking up, moving back into activities with more enthusiasm, beginning to make choices about your life without thinking as much about your parents' divorce, then you are coming into your own again. There really is hope. Not hope that there won't be any more pain, but hope that you can be a mature, healthy person without wounds that incapacitate you.

Part III, containing Chapters 10 through 14, is concerned with actions. There I attempt to make suggestions to you on how to use the experience you have been through for your own good and growth. I don't want you to have to carry unnecessary burdens that will contaminate your life more than is to be expected.

Sadness is a difficult feeling. It tends to slow us down instead of filling us with energy as anger often does. We often feel numb along with the sadness, because we are protecting ourselves from very deep pain.

It is important to let ourselves feel sad. It has a healing effect on us. It is also important that we move on, so that we don't turn sadness into serious depression.

3. Sometimes Glad

At the first meeting I had with a group of teen-agers whose parents had divorced, one of my first questions was, "What kinds of things do you think the book should talk about?" One of the group members replied, "Do you have a section on fear?" When asked to say more about what she meant, she reported that her younger sister had been having nightmares about the possibility of her parents remarrying or of her mother marrying someone else. Her memory of marriage was long nights of loud arguments during which she could not sleep, and she hoped that she would never have to go through that again.

It may seem strange for me to begin a chapter on "being glad" with an example like that, but I think it makes the point very well. For many people, perhaps yourself, the time during which parents lived together was so unhappy, so miserable, that they were relieved when the divorce took place. Regardless of how much pain may be involved around a divorce, there is also a real sense of relief that the difficult moments of interaction are over. And so, there are moments of being glad.

That kind of gladness may best be described as relief. No

more bad scenes! At least, that is the hope. There are some advantages to having only one parent to deal with instead of two. For one thing, the one doesn't have backup support when you are putting on pressure for something you want. For another thing, you don't have to "share" that parent with someone else, if your relationship is particularly important to you.

But there are other kinds of gladness besides relief. One of them is called "denial."

Denial is a more subtle kind of feeling and can be more dangerous. It is a feeling that is "faked" many times. Perhaps the best description is "being cool" about the whole thing, as if it doesn't really matter. If you have found yourself pretending at times that the divorce of your parents really doesn't amount to that much hassle, that you are in charge of yourself and can handle it, be careful! Certainly you don't want to share your problems with everybody, but at the same time there do need to be some places where you can "let your hair down" and admit the problems that come with such an event in your life.

The feeling of being glad is a problem only if you maintain that it is the *only* feeling. And at times it seems necessary to tell people it's all right just in order to protect yourself. Several members of one of the groups with which I met commented on the number of people who, when finding out about a divorce, come over with great curiosity. All kinds of questions are asked about what happened and what it makes you feel like. Those folks are seldom helpful, and it becomes important to protect yourself from them. And sometimes the best defense is to pretend that you are altogether happy about the decision. As I mentioned in the chapter about sadness, there can be a real sense of relief after the divorce takes place. But the feeling of loss is very real also. Glad? Sure. But that's not all. Take a little time now to think about the things you are genuinely glad about in the divorce. And then take a little more time to quiz yourself about things you may be denying by trying to convince yourself that you are glad.

There is another kind of gladness that often comes. A young adult woman whose parents divorced during her late high school and early college years described it this way. "I am, and was, very glad that they were divorced; I don't think it ever would have been possible for me to have any sort of healthy concept of a relationship or marriage had they not." She went on to say that had her parents remained married, the image she would have had of *all* marriages would have been one characterized by the degree of unhappiness, distrust, and pain that she saw while growing up with both of them. Their divorce, in one way, showed that marriage didn't *have* to be like that. In fact, she could then feel free to look at other marriages and evaluate them, instead of somehow being tied to that of her parents as being a typical example.

That is a kind of gladness that lends hope to those who are the sons and daughters of divorced parents. It is a feeling of relief, of release from the bondage of having to defend their situation or having to look at marriage as typically a miserable experience. Being out frees one to look at the various possibilities.

So, gladness is an important source of relief in the midst of very difficult situations. It defends you against those who intrude into your personal life when you didn't invite them.

It says my pain is mine, and I choose which persons will share it with me.

A second function that gladness serves can be less healthy for you. If it becomes something you think you *have* to feel or *ought* to feel in order to prove your own strength and independence, then it can be quite dangerous and leave you quite lonely. Sure, you need time to yourself and feelings that are private, but be careful that you don't isolate yourself from the world altogether.

And third, gladness can provide you with enough distance from the difficult moments for you to look around at your own possibilities in life. That gets us into talking about thinking again and the thoughts you have about your own hopes, fears, and possibilities for marriage. I'll be talking about that more specifically in Chapter 7, and if you wish, you can go on to look at that now if that whets your interest.

Think for a few minutes about the things you feel relieved about because of your parents' divorce. Are you glad for them in particular ways? Are you glad for yourself? What are you glad about? And then join me in the next chapter as I talk a bit about how complicated we human beings are with all those very different feelings racing about inside us, often at the same time.

4. Mostly Mixed

When I first began to write the section on feelings, my outline was longer than it is now. There were discussions of guilt, loneliness, fear, and apathy along with the chapters you have read on anger, sadness, and relief. The more I looked at it, the more it began to look too simple. It had the appearance of a list of options, almost as if some people are mad, others are sad, and so forth. But that, of course, is not the case. We are human beings who experience all of those feelings at various moments, and sometimes they are present in combinations. So, it seemed to me that it was better to pick some of the more obvious ones, fit more subtle ones in, and then remind you that we are not so simply created that feelings come along one at a time. We are mostly mixed.

By mostly mixed I mean that we are very capable, and it is normal, of experiencing many different, indeed opposing, feelings at the same time. It is logical for sadness, depression, and grief to occur at the same points, because they seem to be related to each other. But to experience sadness and gladness at the same time? It doesn't seem to make as much sense, but nevertheless it is so.

So, let me talk with you a bit about what being a normal

person is like. The first thing to bear in mind is that *feelings are not logical,* and we don't have that much control over them. It is very easy for us to both love and be angry with the same person at the same time. Logically, that doesn't make much sense. After all, if you are angry with someone, why should you be caring about that person? The person has offended you, or deprived you, or treated you unjustly. So, anger? Yes. But still care? Yes. There is no real explanation for that, but it is so.

One of the best examples that comes to mind is an encounter I had with my seven-year-old daughter just a week before I wrote this chapter. My wife and I had gone away for a week, and our daughter had stayed at home with a student couple whom she knew and who took care of her, got her to school, etc. We noticed her sadness at our leaving, and when we returned there was a very hectic afternoon. When I got home and attempted to hug her, she turned and raced into the next room, sat down on the couch with her back to me. No responses would she make to any of my questions: "Allison, are you mad about something?" "Were you sad about our going away?"

When I tried to hug her, she jerked away and made it known that I was to stay clear. I sat in the room with her for a while, and after what seemed a long time, I remembered something. I said to her: "You know, I remember once when I was a little boy and my parents went away for a while. When they came back, I was so glad to have them back. But at the same time I was furious with them for leaving me, and I couldn't decide what to say to them."

She looked up at me very slowly, said, "Yeah," and

bounded across the room into my arms, bursting into tears as she came.

Mixed feelings. She was furious with me. She loved me. And that was the way I found myself feeling toward her. I was so glad to see her, and I was mad at her for not acting glad to see me. That is the normal state for us human beings during tough times in our lives.

And that is the normal state for you. You can love your parents very much and, at the same time, be intensely angry with them for what you experience their decision to be doing to you. As one daughter of divorced parents put it to me: "I was a walking time bomb of anger, frustration, and self-righteousness. . . . I felt I was needed. . . . I didn't feel they loved me." All those very different experiences flowing around inside us are very confusing. No wonder we lose confidence in ourselves during such times. After all, we have been taught the importance of being determined, self-assured, focused, and confident. Inside we feel hopeful and despairing, angry and loving, sad and glad, responsible and not responsible. As another person put it: "I could both understand and disagree with the action [the divorce]. . . . A happy and sad scar."

A very helpful person in bringing us understanding of this was Sigmund Freud. In describing the development of the child, he noted the period in which the child feels deeply dependent on and loving of the parent. At the same time, the child becomes resentful of the "interference" of the parent with what the child wants to do. Especially does this come into focus when the child wants to get the sole affection of, say, the parent of the opposite sex. Most of us have gone through the period in our younger years of wanting to marry the parent of the opposite sex for ourselves. At any rate, the parent of the same sex then becomes a "competitor" for the warmth and attention of the other parent. "If only this competitor were out of the way," we say to ourselves in one way or another. Yet, at the same time, we think how sad and grieved we would be if that other person were to leave or somehow be removed from our lives forever or for a long period of time.

Thus, says Freud, comes the beginning of the experience of guilt. We have evil thoughts about a person for whom we care very much. What must be wrong with me? we think when such thoughts or feelings flash through our minds. Yet, Freud tells us, such experiences are normal to the human condition. It would be more unusual for us *not* to have such feelings.

And so the process continues throughout our lives. Mixed feelings about parents, mixed feelings about ourselves, mixed feelings about the events in our lives, mixed feelings about just about anything. The problem is that we have often been taught that we *shouldn't* have such mixed feelings, and so we feel guilty when both are present.

One mother told me of the occasion when she and her husband planned how to tell their three boys that they were going to divorce. She had read the books that told her that children often feel responsible for the divorce, thinking that their own bad feelings and thoughts may have somehow contaminated the relationship of two persons whom they love very much. In the cases of the three children, each came to her at separate times to tell her that they were sorry for having misbehaved, having expressed anger, etc., and thus were fearful that they had caused the divorce to take place. Mixed feelings—I am responsible, I am not responsible. All at the same time.

All this is to say that when your parents divorce, you are *sure* to have mixed feelings. Angry? Yes. Sad? Yes. Glad? Yes. And probably lots more. The danger is that you will slip into thinking that you *ought* to be one way or another and then will feel even worse when you find that you *can't* feel just one way. They are all there.

What you can do is begin to sort out the feelings, admit to them all, survey yourself to see if you are ignoring any of them. But that is not enough. Then you can begin to see what *effects* those feelings are having on you. Are they leading you to cut off relationships that are important to you? Are they leading you to get into relationships that aren't really that attractive? Are you trying to feel a particular way because one of your parents or someone else *wants* you to? Stop and think about those questions for a while. Your answers about that will lead us into the next section of my book. You see, we can't choose our feelings, but we can make choices about what we *do* about them.

In summary, when your parents divorce, they are experiencing a lot of mixed feelings, too. Their hope is that you won't have to go through the agony which they are having. So, they may, out of good motivation, lay some difficult demands on you. "Don't be angry with us. We tried hard." That is an impossible demand. You are probably going to be resentful, at least for a time. "Don't judge us for what we have done." "Don't let what we are doing affect you." "Don't let it get to you." Keep in mind that those are wishes, not commands. Even if they sound like commands, you can't meet them. What you have to decide is not whether you feel all those things, but whether you will let your parents know that you feel those things. That's where some decisions have to be made. They are decisions that you must make about your welfare and about their welfare. And that is true not only at the time of the divorce but with regard to all the years that are to come in which you will have some kind of relationship with them.

That is what I want to talk with you about in Part III. What are the *effects* that all these feelings have on you? I hope that you will take one more moment to look over the various feelings that you have had and are having now before we move on.

PART
II
THOUGHTS

5. Divorce and the Church

As you may remember, I am a Presbyterian minister. One of my concerns in writing this book is to be helpful to folks like yourself who are having to deal with all the issues of the divorce of their parents. This, to me, is a vital concern of the church as well. As a minister I have tried to make time available to both parents and children when divorce seems possible or is already accomplished. In addition, the church in which I last served held, and still does hold, a regular group for divorced persons to talk and plan the ways in which they will deal with their lives now and in the future. The church ought to be involved in this, because part of its mission is caring for those who are going through difficult moments in their lives.

Unfortunately, many people have other views of the church. One of those views has been that divorce is wrong and that those who divorce should be confronted with their wrongdoings. The motivation can be understood as a desire to emphasize the importance of marriage and family life. But one of the side effects can be that divorced persons *and their children* feel unwelcome in the church. It is viewed in terms of its judgment rather than in terms of its concern to help persons in their healing from wounds brought about by experiences such as divorce.

What I would like to do in this chapter is explain a more positive view of the church's involvement in divorce. Remember that this is the first chapter in a section on thoughts, and some thoughts about a view of divorce from a church perspective may be helpful to you in your own thinking.

To begin, the Bible itself places very high importance on relationships. Genesis, the first book in the Old Testament, tells the story of creation and in the second chapter reports the view of God that it is not good for humans to be alone (Gen. 2:18). And so there is the creation of a "partner." The purpose? So that they can share in the enjoyment and ruling of the creation that God has provided. From that point on you can find case after case of spots where relationships have gone sour and failed. At the same time, you can find case after case of beauty in relationships that illustrate how good they *can* be. In fact, marriage is often used as an example of what the relationship between God and persons is intended to be.

As a result of that emphasis on the *intention* for relationships, the church has always placed a strong concern on marriage. And, because of the comparison between marital partners and the partnership of God and persons, there has been a strong emphasis on fidelity and permanence in marriage. Divorce obviously took place frequently in Old Testament times, and there are many laws that stipulate what is to happen in such cases. The New Testament, as well, discusses divorce at several points.

When you read about divorce in the Bible and in the

history of the church, you often find the word "sin" lurking somewhere in the vicinity. And the use of that word "sin" in connection with divorce has resulted in what many people view as a judgmental and punitive attitude on the part of the church.

I'd like you to think with me for a few minutes on what that word "sin" means. The literal translation of it from the Greek has to do with "missing the mark." The word has original reference to a marksman shooting an arrow at a target, and when the center of the target is missed, then the bowman has sinned.

Now, that concept provides some very helpful understanding of the way in which divorce can, and in my opinion *should,* be viewed. When two persons marry and then divorce, they have "fallen short" of the mark, of the intention. The marriage has not been what such a union is intended to be for those two persons. That certainly is a judgment. The view is that they have not been willing or able to live up to their promises. The task of the church is, on the one hand, to show people what marriage is intended to be. The hope is that, by teaching *what* it is and *how* to nurture it, marriages will succeed. Success means that two persons can love each other, share their lives, provide partnership and companionship in enjoying the pleasures and comforting each other during the rough times. And the church should provide encouragement to husbands and wives to work things out, if possible, when things go badly. Why? Because it is God's intention and our hope that marriage will be a rich experience for the persons involved.

The more ticklish part is how the church responds to those who do divorce, who do fall short of the mark. One option, obviously, is to be highly critical of them for "failing." For me, the more important option is to recognize the disappointment and pain that go on in two persons who have made a commitment to each other and found that it has not worked. *They* experience themselves as having failed, and what is needed is encouragement and forgiveness rather than punishment and criticism.

The message of the New Testament is that we are to take our responsibilities very seriously, but when we fall short, there is grace and reassurance to support us as we try to repair the damage and move on.

The church, then, should be a place that encourages those who are married to continue to grow. *And* it is a place where support and encouragement are available to those for whom marriage has "fallen short" of what it was hoped to be. Furthermore, it should be a place for the sons and daughters of divorced parents to find friends, counseling, encouragement, and acceptance. It should be a place that gives you some enjoyable moments to "step outside" of having to think about what has happened to you. It should also be a place that gives you the opportunity to look carefully at what has happened to you and how you will respond to it.

The reason I am telling you all this is twofold. First, I would like a church to be one of the places where you can look for support and encouragement during some of the tough times in your dealing with your parents' divorce.

The second part of my motivation is more than advertising the church as a place to go. I have found that this view of divorce is helpful to me in understanding and thinking about what happens. You see, admitting that divorce is a disappointment and a failure is much more realistic than trying to pretend that it doesn't matter or that everything about it was for the best. At the same time, something being a failure doesn't mean that we have to pay a price for it the rest of our lives. It can be an opportunity for you to learn more about yourself and to make decisions about your own life that you might not have even thought about. Just as with the feelings I talked about in Part I, the view of the church acknowledges that the picture is *mixed!*

One of the persons whom I hope you can talk with about your parents' divorce is your pastor. We can agree readily that some pastors are better than others, and there will be some whom you just don't feel free to turn to for such a conversation. But my hope is that there is one around to whom you can go, even if not at a church with which you are connected.

Many churches are showing more interest in designing programs to help people understand what goes on in a divorce and the effects it has on the various family members. Perhaps there is a regular group meeting that you can attend. I found many folks who were willing to meet to discuss this book while it was being written, and I hope it was helpful to them to talk about it as well as being helpful to me. Perhaps there are programs at which you could talk to other people to let them know what you see the needs to be in a church for the sons and daughters of divorced parents. Helping each other is the name of the game in the church, if the church is truly caring.

Take a few minutes now to think about what I have been saying. Are there any opportunities at your church that might be helpful to you? Are there any spots where you could help the church to be more caring for people such as yourself? What do you think about the view of divorce that I have outlined briefly? Does it help you to think more about what happened?

I would like you to think about divorce as "falling short." Go through some of your thoughts about what marriage and family life ought to be, from your point of view. Wherein did life in your family fall short?

Then, think about the kinds of encouragement you have received since the news of your parents' divorce got out. Has the encouragement been helpful, or did you think there was a subtle, or perhaps overt, disapproval behind it? What kinds of encouragement do you wish you had gotten but didn't?

As you think about these things, perhaps some thoughts about your own views of marriage have come to mind. That is the concern I want to deal with in Chapter 7.

6. Accept What Happened

Along with all the powerful feelings that can take place in response to the divorce of your parents, there also comes a need to understand what happened. The understanding doesn't always explain why the split took place, but you can gain some insight into the process by which it happened. All too often you may be able to remember specific events that took place, and you figured that things were pretty bad. The entire process, however, was probably veiled at many points.

My intention in writing this chapter is to give you some sort of framework within which to look at the events of your parents' process of divorcing. It is a compilation of research that has been done in many areas. I am indebted primarily to Wayne Oates, the editor of this series, for first exposing me to the concept. Since that time my own work has involved me with divorcing partners frequently enough to fill out my own understanding of the process.

As with the stages of grief, there are stages through which a relationship goes when it is coming apart. It is important for you to understand that any relationship has conflict and differences that occur with regularity. People are different, and when any two decide to live together in the closeness of marriage those differences come up. From the place to squeeze the toothpaste tube, to the way to manage the money, to the ways to raise the children, there are expectable disagreements. In a healthy relationship, the tension comes up frequently so that things don't have a chance to escalate because of festering. In fact, they may come up with such regularity that they don't even appear to be conflictual. An issue is mentioned, the possibilities (or different preferences) as to how it should be handled are mentioned, and some decision is made. The hallmark of the health is that the issue is aired, it is dealt with alone, and other distracting elements do not intrude in a complicating fashion.

I. Attack

However, if the relationship is under stress, something very different happens when an issue is brought to the attention of the two partners. Rather than the issue being dealt with directly, it is *used* as an opportunity for one or both partners to attack the other. The attack may occur in various forms. One way, of course, is to tell the other person that his or her view is stupid. That is not an evaluation or a consideration of the view, it is an insult. An insult triggers anger rather than consideration, and so the battle begins.

Another variant is to bring up several issues at the same time. The objective or the result is to overwhelm the person, effectively seeing to it that no resolution takes place. Instead, you find out how much the other person can take. Good strategy for a battle, but poor strategy for a marriage.

Insults, multiple issues, refusal to discuss, sulking silence —all are evidence that a relationship has shifted into a stage of deterioration. Health is covered over rapidly, wounds are struck, and healing often comes slowly.

Stress can bring on this stage. A new job, concerns about the children, problems with money, taking on too many community responsibilities, nosy neighbors or relatives—all these and more can be sources that bring a good relationship to a rugged period. And often the big problem is fatigue. The world you and I live in keeps us pretty busy, and parents are as vulnerable as we are. But that's where the problems can begin. And if this stage of attack continues for too long, there is danger that things will stay that way—or get worse! A typical argument in this stage of attack won't stick with one subject. Within a few minutes the two partners may move from money to sex to children to relatives to—who knows what? That's the difference between healthy tension and the unhealthy kind: the first will stick with one subject and try to work it out; the second covers so many issues that nothing can be worked out.

II. Withdrawal

If things continue in the stage of attack for very long, someone pulls out. Some people will move to this stage very quickly. Attack is too hurtful for them. Others may take years to do so, and those years are the ones remembered so painfully by many children of divorced parents.

Withdrawal is a retreat into distance. It doesn't mean that someone moves out of the house. But it may mean that these persons don't stay at home as much. Perhaps they travel more, have a job that keeps them out late, or their clubs and service organizations demand more time away. All those duties may be real, but now the mother or father (or both!) become more willing to be gone than once was the case.

Finding excuses to be away from home is not the only way to withdraw. It can be done right at home. More time spent in front of the television. Work to do in the basement. Somehow the two persons just don't wind up in the same room together very often. Conversation is confined to business and seldom is fun or concerned with things to do together.

Sometimes it's hard to know whether things are just in a "busy spell" or whether there is a stage of withdrawal going on. You almost have to sense which it is. Perhaps just an atmosphere of tension or unhappiness is all that can be sensed. This stage is harder to live in, in some ways, than the stage of attack. At least when the attacks were on, you *knew* what was happening. In the stage of withdrawal, nothing is out in the open. It just doesn't feel as though things are right.

This can be a very depressing time for the one who is withdrawing. You may have found the person sitting and staring out of the window; perhaps there were some tears. At other times there may have been a kind of frustrating anger going on. There was unhappiness, but no clear reason for it. But you could tell the person's mind was on something else.

Perhaps this is a good place to point out that attacks and withdrawal are not necessarily a sign that a marriage is going bad. Everyone goes through phases like this when some disagreement has occurred that is difficult to solve. Ordinarily, however, the stage doesn't last very long, and things return to normal. These stages are real danger signals if one or both parents stay in them for a very long time and steadily move on to worse stages.

III. THIRD PARTY INVOLVEMENT

Up until now the stages through which unhappy marriage partners move have been relatively private. Perhaps because of embarrassment, they haven't told anyone, often not even the children. In fact, many people who have been through this process are surprised that someone noticed the changes they went through. But if you were on the home scene to any extent at all, you saw them!

This third stage is the point at which people "go public." The loneliness of the withdrawn stage becomes too much to bear, and the search is on for someone to understand their unhappiness. You may have been chosen to be the third party. Your father or mother may have come to you privately and spoken of being very unhappy. There may even be some mention of divorce at this point, but it is difficult to tell how serious the marriage problem is. The main need is for someone else to listen and to understand.

Of course, there are many other third parties to whom someone may turn. Other relatives or friends may be the choice. Unfortunately, the choice may be someone to "substitute" in some way for the spouse. The substitution may be someone to talk to, or it may go as far as an affair with varying levels of sexual involvement. The search for a third party is an attempt to find someone to meet the needs no longer being met in the marriage. Those needs are many, and some will be more important to one person than another.

Another option for a third party is professional help of some kind. A minister, a psychologist, a physician and/or psychiatrist, family counselors—all of these and more are available to folks who come to the point of being able to ask for help.

The kind of third party chosen makes a great deal of difference in the chances of the marriage surviving. Of course, time makes a big difference also. Staying too long in those stages of attack or withdrawal can leave such deep wounds that it is very difficult to repair the damage. Talking to family may result in people "choosing up sides" to the degree that more hostility is around than can be managed. Having an affair, or finding a substitute of some kind often lessens the interest in repairing the marriage. Sometimes, however, the affair can be such a shock that new interest comes in making things right in the marriage again. The choice of a counselor can be very critical as well. Will there be encouragement to work things out or to separate? Trust in the counselor is important, as well as motivation to really work on the relationship. In a later chapter, I will talk about some ways to evaluate counselors, in case you have considered seeing one yourself.

IV. Serious Threats

Depending on the third party situation, a great deal can happen. If things worsen, more serious thought is given to ending the marriage. Threats may have been made frequently in the stage of attacks. In this stage, the threats are more serious, and they are acted upon.

An attorney may be consulted. One parent may move out of the house. Clear plans begin to be made. The children are more formally notified that divorce is a real possibility.

This may be a time in which things become more calm, as if the decision were already made. Or, on the other hand, things may be very frantic. The threats may be a last-ditch attempt to reverse the decline and save the marriage. In any case, it is a very difficult period for sons and daughters.

V. Divorce

The phase of actual divorce is not short. Court procedures can be long. In some states, for instance, there must be a certain period of separation before the divorce can be final. As with the preceding stage, the situation may be very calm or it may be hysterical.

Some people seem to use this phase to repeat the stage of attack. In states where fault must be established, the husband and wife make strong accusations about each other, and use the legal procedure to hurt each other. In stages where that is not allowed, there may be a battle over the custody of the children. Then, one partner can charge the other with being an "unfit parent." This is a particularly difficult period if you are the one caught in the middle. Depending on your age, the court may call on you to express your preference about the custody and visiting arrangements.

Various money matters and the distribution of property must be agreed upon or settled by the court. If agreement about the spending of money has always been a problem, it may well be very difficult here as well.

For other marriages, the legal phase is very quick and matter-of-fact. The battles are over. The decisions have been made. The husband and wife want to settle it as quickly as possible.

VI. GRIEF

Grief may be the surprise element for many people. It probably isn't for you. After a divorce is finalized, many partners go into a period of sadness or depression about what has happened. They are having to deal with many difficult decisions and new circumstances because of the divorce. Furthermore, even if they do not grieve the loss of their spouse, they are very disappointed and hurt that the marriage did not turn out to be what they hoped for. You might want to review the stages of grief I discussed in the chapter on sadness to remind you of what this is like for them. It is very much the same as it was, and is, for you.

I hope that these descriptions of what often happens in the deterioration of a marriage are helpful to you. Obviously, they don't explain why the marriage didn't work. I'm not sure that anyone can ever answer that question.

The stages are helpful to me in being able to describe a

little more accurately what happened. And seeing that what happens centers so much on the way people handle their differences will, I hope, relieve you of any fears you have about having some responsibility for what happened.

Perhaps it would be helpful for you to take some time to think now about these stages and whether they seem to describe what you have seen and wondered about many times. I hope you will take some time to do that.

7. My Own Marriage

The divorce of parents certainly affects a child's view of marriage. Whatever your age now, whatever your age at the time of your parents' divorce, you now have some views about marriage that have been shaped significantly by that experience. As one person described it, immediately after her parents' divorce had taken place, "Marriage would never be in the cards for me, and every other woman was a fool to subject herself to such a demeaning and suicidal arrangement." Now, some years later, that same person writes: "I suppose on the whole I have a very high regard toward marriage now. I respect the commitment and what I think could be a very close communication between two people for them to feel fulfilled within the institution."

Those thoughts reflect a process that one person has gone through in dealing with divorce in her life. What effects do you see the experience having on your thinking about marriage—your own and marriage generally?

I know that the audience addressed in this book includes persons in their teens who have not even considered a marriage partner yet. It also includes young adults who are presently married. So, my question is directed to all of you.

61

If you haven't chosen a partner yet, what kind of person are you looking for? If you are married now, how were you influenced in your choice of a partner, and how does your parents' divorce affect your present relationship with your spouse?

There are several areas we should think about in this chapter. They all have to do with relationships with people, but let's try to take them one at a time.

The first has to do with thoughts that you have about men. Notice that I am using the word "thoughts" instead of "feelings." We will want to consider feelings as well, but I want to encourage you first to take a look at the regard you have for males. This is an examination I want you to make whether you are a male or a female.

To start off, what images come to mind when you think about a man? Do they have to do with physical appearance? Are they related to what men do? What kinds of feelings do you think are typical of men?

I do a great deal of premarital and marital counseling. One of the things that strikes me so often in conversations with people is the assumptions they make about what men (or women) are like. Usually that assumption is based on what their own father or some significant male was, or is, like. For instance, if your father tended to be gone a lot, and if, when home, he was tired and didn't talk very much, your assumption may be that most men don't hang around home much and aren't very helpful when they do. Certainly, when you think about it you know better than that, but the first assumption, your expectation, may be that "most men are like that."

Why is that an important thing for you to look at? If you

are a female, marriage may not look very attractive if that is what men are like. Or, if you do choose to get married, you won't expect very much from a husband. That will have a great deal to do with how you view marriage.

If you are a male, that same image of what a father/husband is like sets you with some expectations, too. You may wonder why you should bother with getting married if you wouldn't hang around much anyway. Or you may figure that a marriage is something to be used for your own convenience and nothing more.

Those are just some examples of how your feelings about men may affect your future views about marriage. Your experience may have been different. A father may have been very warm and compassionate, always willing to take time. If so, that can become the expectation you have of all men, and discovering otherwise may be a real shock.

Everyone goes through such formation of expectations with regard to men. But the divorce of your parents often results in your looking more deeply. Your curiosity is raised, along with your pain, to find out what went wrong and to form some lasting impressions of what to expect in your own future.

The same, of course, is true of expectations about women. What was, or is, your mother like? Warm? Available? Aloof? Always tired and irritable? Critical of herself? Critical of men? These and other characteristics become formative impressions and thoughts about what women are like and what they have to deal with in life. If you are a woman, that teaches you some things about the life of females that you will need to check out time and time again. If you are a man, that influences what you expect women to be like generally and thus leads you to make decisions, *before you ever enter a new relationship,* about how to treat and care for them.

Many, many books have dealt with discussions of the influences that mothers and fathers have on their children's feelings about themselves and other men and women. I don't want to take you on a long trip about that. What I do want to do is to impress on you the importance of taking a look at what your parents' marriage and divorce has done to your own thinking about yourself and your potential spouse, if you are even inclined to think about marriage for yourself.

One way to approach your own thoughts about marriage is to sit down and conduct an imaginary discussion between several persons. First, listen to the words you think your father would say to you about marriage. What would be his message to you about what to expect? Secondly, listen to what you think your mother would say. Where are the messages the same? Where do they differ? The third part of the conversation would involve your brothers, your sisters, and close friends of the family, whoever they may be. What would they say marriage does to people and for people?

Now comes the most important part of the conversation. What are your contributions to this event? Based on what you have seen of your parents' marriage, what would you say it is like? What has it done to and for you? What would you have changed about it? If you were going to teach a course on marriage, what would it present?

While you are thinking about these questions, I would like to give you a few more ideas. They come from my own understanding of what marriage is *intended* to be. They come from the study I have done in the Bible and theology, and much of my thought is built around trying to understand the meaning of "partner" in Genesis 2:18. This is the record of the creation of the woman, which is done because God says, "It is not good for the man to be alone, so I will make him a partner." That verse is very important in the church's understanding of what marriage was, and is, intended to be.

The Hebrew for "partner" can also be translated "help-meet" or "helpmate," but what is important is the definition of the word. There are three defining characteristics.

First, the partners are *equal.* Neither one is more important or more powerful than the other. No status battles should be present in their relationship. In the sight of God, and in each other's sight, they are *both* vital to the relationship. Furthermore, neither has the right to *use* the other like property or as a subordinate who is expected to obey orders. And, most important, since they are equal, they are to care for each other as much as each cares for himself or herself. Very important.

Second, the partners are *adequate* for each other. They each have needs that can be met by the partner. Perhaps the needs are for security and comfort. Perhaps the needs are for sexual enjoyment. Also, there are needs for one to "take over" during times when the other is weak, or preoccupied, or ill. The important issue is that these persons have the *capacity* to be responsible *for* each other and responsible *to* each other. They can be faithful, and should be, in many, many ways.

Third, the partners are *different* from each other. Just because they are equal and adequate does not mean that they are the same. Their needs may be very different. Their capabilities may be very different, as may be their interests.

But those very differences make the possibility of their taking care of each other even more comprehensive. Furthermore, since they are different and changing, they never will understand each other fully! Reading each other's mind isn't very dependable. Those differences can be the cause of great conflict, or they can be the basis for the two being fascinated and interested in each other for a long, long time. It depends on how adept they are at dealing with differences.

The intent of marriage is for enjoyment of each other and to provide a context in which two persons can be secure and mature. We certainly know that this is not always what happens! The danger is that we will take the failure of a marriage as our idea or model for what marriage is like generally.

I hope you will think about these characteristics which I have described briefly. Use them in evaluating what happened in your parents' marriage. More importantly, use them and what you have learned in thinking about your own marriage, now or in the future.

My greatest hope is that you won't use your parents' divorce to decide whether you will or won't get married. I would like you to use their experience as an education for yourself. It's an education that teaches you to be very, very careful in choosing a spouse. A relationship can be very enjoyable and fulfilling in many ways, but that doesn't mean that it will make a marriage.

Formulate some questions that you will use to evaluate a prospective mate. The question is not whether or not to marry. It is whether or not a particular person offers the opportunity for the two of you to experience each other as equal, adequate, and different.

There may be a good bit of baggage you will have to deal with before you can make an evaluation like that. Taking a hard look at your thoughts about men, women, and marriage is one step in doing just that.

8. New Marriages for My Parents?

Whenever a divorce occurs, the possibility of a new marriage is there automatically. In fact, it is quite likely. As one person cleverly put it, "Eighty percent of divorces end up in marriage!" So, as if there weren't enough factors for the sons and daughters of divorce to deal with, here is one more. For some of you, the thought of a remarriage is a relief. For others, it is to be dreaded. What are some of the factors that come into play here, and how do they affect our thinking?

You may remember, from the chapter on "Sometimes Glad," the young girl who had nightmares about the possibility of her mother marrying again. That daughter's experience of marriage had been an emotional nightmare for her on many occasions, so the thought of another marriage was frightening to her. She illustrates well the response of considering marriage, any marriage, to be a bad deal. When your own experience of the only marriage you have known closely for a long period of time is a bad one, it is difficult to think of a new marriage as being a good deal, regardless of the amount of good things your mother or father says about it. That's one of the major factors that affect our thinking about a new marriage—what experiences might be repeated that we would just as soon not have to go through again.

A second factor that affects us deeply is what we may lose by such an event. For instance, if you are still living with the parent who is about to marry, you will lose the amount of warmth, time, and influence you have had while living with that parent alone. You will have to share in ways that were not necessary before. I don't want you to think of this in terms of right or wrong for the moment. The more important issue is that *it is a fact* that you will not have the same relationship with that parent.

This is true whether you are living with that parent or not. The new marriage means that another person will now play some part in making decisions, whereas before, decisions were made *only* by your mother or father, if you are still of an age when such decisions are being made. Even if you are no longer living with a parent or are old enough that no decisions are being made about you, when phone calls are made you will talk to two persons now instead of one. You will be expected to be interested in the welfare of the new partner, whether you had any interest in the person previously or not. Of course, knowing the person for a while before the marriage takes place helps.

A third factor has to do with that process of sadness, or grief, which I discussed in Chapter 2. When the new marriage is announced or takes place, many people experience again their sadness that the first marriage didn't work. The remarriage means that now it is impossible, or at least unlikely, that the original parents will resolve their differences and marry each other again. In that sense, the new marriage means that the death of the old one is complete. And for many of you, the secret hope that things would eventually work out is now gone forever.

Of course, a fourth factor may well be that the new marriage will be good for them and for you. The new partner brings some of those qualities of a marriage into your life and the life of your parent that have not been around for a long time, if they ever were. And that means things improve for you as well.

We can't think of these various factors as a list of choices, of which one will fit you. They will come in combinations ordinarily. For instance, I can remember with surprise my reaction when my father first announced that he was going to remarry. My mother had died several years prior, and I was aware that loneliness was very difficult for him. What I had expected to feel when he told me of his plans was happiness. And I did experience a real surge of joy for him. I had known my stepmother for several years, liked her, and was happy for both of them.

The surprise for me was that, along with my happiness for them, I found myself grieving over the death of my mother again. You see, the news was good and bad. Good that they were finding happiness. Bad in that this was a further reminder that my mother really was dead.

Of course, my experience came out of the experience of a remarriage following the deaths of the spouses of both my father and my stepmother. But I think, and many have told me, that the experience is much the same for a new marriage following a divorce. The feelings and the thoughts are mixtures of pleasure and pain, rejoicing and grieving that life has brought these people to this particular place.

I have written primarily of the effects that a new marriage

has on you—what you may lose, what you may gain, what you may experience. Perhaps the most important issue in all of this, however, is the *power* that you have in the situation. For you can exert a great deal of influence and pressure that will affect the marriage very directly. This is a spot where you must make some very important decisions as you struggle with what is in this marriage for them and what is in it for you.

I plan to talk more about your behavior or actions in Part III. But it is very important here for you to see how necessary it is to do some thinking about all this so that your actions will be consistent with what you want for them and for yourself.

When the divorce of your parents took place, that was a very powerless time for you. Two of the most important persons in your life were making a decision that would affect you for a long time and you had very little to do with it. Depending on your age, you may have taken more or less responsibility for the divorce. There is a need for us to "have a part" in something that affects us that deeply. It gives us a sense of power or control to think that we do. But when you get right down to it, you had no real influence in your parents' decision to divorce.

Furthermore, when arrangements were being made about places where you would live, custody, plans for vocation, etc., you were still at a low level of power, depending on your age and the degree to which you were allowed to participate. In a real sense, you have had to live with decisions other people made on your behalf.

Now, however, with the coming of a new marriage, you *can have* a great deal to do with what happens. Your support of the marriage can help them a great deal. Your undercutting of it can do a great deal of harm to it.

What about them? What do you want for them? What do you see their needs and hopes to be in this new venture —a venture that carries with it the knowledge that a previous marriage failed? It is a venture that often carries with it a determination to "make this one work." You have to make some decisions *in your thinking* about the degree to which you will support them in this relationship.

What about you? What do you want for yourself as this new marriage takes place? What are the things you need and want that perhaps have not been possible before? Are you willing to talk about them out loud? Do you need to think about it some more just to get a clear idea of what is at stake for you in this new relationship?

One mother told me of the deep disappointment that her children experienced when their father remarried. They lived with her but had visited with their father three weekends a month and for two months of the summer. The visits were good ones for them, and they had always looked forward to their time with him. But after his remarriage, the visits declined rapidly. His new wife had her own children, and he became more involved with them and less involved with his. The visits dropped to once a month and even less frequently.

Another divorced parent told me of the positive benefits that came from remarriage. The children were getting another view of marriage, a more positive one. In fact, after the remarriage of both parents, there was a greater willingness to talk with the children about what had happened in the divorce and what they were attempting to do with the new partners to "see to it" that the marriages this time would last.

You, because of your age, have more power than smaller children do to exercise your rights to play a part in helping a new relationship to work. Of course, some parents will be more receptive to your involvement than others. But as a person at an age when significant relationships become more and more important, it is important for you to learn from a new marriage. Initiate conversation about what you hope for them and for yourself. Talk about what you want your relationship with them to be. And that means all the way from what you will call your stepparent, to the expressions of caring, to the amount of time you want with both of them and separately. It can be a positive experience for you in your own growth—and in theirs!

9. Where Do I Belong?

The last major thought I would like to talk about with you is "home." Where is it and what is it for you? Divorce throws that concept up into the air for us many times. A twenty-year-old woman told me at the time of her parents' divorce, "The saddest thing for me is that I don't feel like I have a home anymore." Her concept of home was the place where her parents lived together. Now they were no longer together, neither of them lived in the house she was familiar with when growing up, neither lived in the town where she grew up with friends. When she wanted to go home, where was it?

Robert Frost once wrote something to the effect that home was the place where, if you had to go there, they had to take you in. But that doesn't encompass the bounds of home once a divorce has occurred. What if there are several places, all unfamiliar because of different house, different place, and different occupants?

Also, home can be a place that reminds you of being "torn up" rather than a place to which you go for security and comfort. The problem of "them versus me" comes up too in the thoughts about where home *is* for you and where your parents *want* home to be for you.

There are various complicating factors that go into our thinking about home. The most important thing to me in writing this chapter is to help you do some thinking about *your* definition of what you want your home to be. Then, in the next few chapters, I am going to talk about some of the things that you can do to help shape a home where you can feel at home.

One thing that influences you very much in your *thinking* about a home is how you *feel* when you are at a particular place. Our feelings are affected by what other people want or expect of us. So, if *both* parents are exerting pressure on you to think of them or their house as your home, there's a problem. As one member of a group of sons and daughters of divorced parents put it, "Every time a holiday comes around, you have to decide which parent to desert." When the parent you are leaving to go visit the other evidences hurt and loneliness, it makes it very difficult for you to feel at home in either place. When you are away from that parent, you feel guilty. When you are with that parent, you feel resentful that the parent wants you to be "happier" there than with the other. Of course, those wishes don't have to be said to you out loud. You can sense them through facial expressions and voice tones. With feelings like those flying around, it becomes difficult for you to think of yourself as having a home in the deeper sense of the word, because there isn't a place where you can feel comfortable.

A second influence on your thinking of your *home* involves the people who are there. I wrote in the previous chapter about the effects of a new marriage. The most obvious one, of course, is that a new person comes into your life, living in close quarters with you, with whom you have to cooperate to some degree in establishing a life-style that you can all exist in together. This, of course, presumes that you are living there fairly continuously. But even visits for short periods of time are affected by this relatively unknown new person in your life. Several members of various groups have commented that the situation is "not so bad" if the stepparent is known previously. There has been time for adjustment.

A third factor is what gets talked about around the place. Is there freedom for you to deal with the issues that concern you? Or are there certain subjects or persons that should not be brought up in any conversations? On the other hand, are there subjects and persons brought up by the others in the house on a constant basis, issues that are uncomfortable or distasteful to you to hear about over and over again? An extreme example, but not unusual, is the father who constantly asks you what your mother has been doing. Or the mother who constantly points out the shortcomings and failures of your father. Of course, the roles can be reversed. Such unpleasantness, such "putting you in the middle," makes it very difficult for you to consider that place a home. Instead, it becomes a place of pressure and discomfort.

Fourth, it is difficult to feel at home if you are moving all the time. Living out of a suitcase is not unusual for many children of divorce. Out of a concern to provide "equal time," all too often children are shuttled back and forth constantly. The result is "equal time" all right, but it is accompanied by their having to manage two sets of friends, two sets of behavioral expectations, two rooms, two diets, and multiple other factors that make it hard to feel "settled." Constant arrangements, changing of plans, trying to mediate disputes between parents can result in a rather nomadic existence and the sense of not having a home but simply passing through.

These four factors have been talked about thus far in fairly negative terms, but they can be turned around easily. After all, changes may well have been for the better in terms of the experiences you have had. Your feelings may be more settled because of the absence of conflict. The people with whom you now live may well be more to your liking, and for the first time in your life you may find freedom to talk, tease, laugh, and engage in serious conversation without threat of bad endings. The conversation has focus, and any moving back and forth that goes on may be enjoyable. In fact, the relationship with both parents may be better because of their not being locked in conflict or avoidance of each other.

More likely than not, however, your experience is a mixture of the good and the bad. And home is best characterized as different. The greatest change that has taken place in your idea of home is that it is *different* and will always be so. New feelings, new place, new people, new concerns, and new style of living. For most folks, changing is uncomfortable. We usually prefer to remain reasonably the same in most areas of our lives and to experience change in only a few at a time. Divorce brings everything up for change all at once.

With that change going on or having gone on around you, there is opportunity to make some decisions of your own. And Part III will attempt to deal with what some of those actions may be.

PART
III
ACTIONS

10. Consider the Options

I intend this chapter to be quite brief. It is designed to be a reminder of several items mentioned in Part II on thoughts and perspectives. This section, Part III, is intended to deal with decisions and actions. It comes in this order, because constructive action comes out of careful reflection on one's feelings and thoughts. A psychiatrist friend of mine was fond of saying that all people feel, think, and act. They have no control over their feelings. If something unjust is done to you, you feel angry whether you like the feeling or not. You have pretty good control over your thoughts. In other words, thinking is often done intentionally. We try to work on things in an orderly way in thinking and watch for logic and propriety in what we reason out. Thus, if someone treats you unjustly, you feel angry, but you can then begin to explain or think about the person's action in an attempt to make sense out of it and to help yourself feel differently about it. You do have control over your actions. Even though we can't help feeling angry, and we find it hard to arrive at a reasonable explanation, we can decide *not to* do something hostile in return. So, you don't teach people not to feel angry, because they can't control that. You teach people not to do hostile things that could get them in trouble.

Well, the purpose of that digression is to point out where we have been coming in the order of this book. Part I dealt with those aspects of ourselves over which we have little control—our feelings. Part II dealt with thinking, our need to explain and understand the events that have taken place in our lives. Now we come to the spot over which you have the most control. "What are you going to do about it?"

If what you decide to do is going to be as constructive as possible, it will be based on careful attention to the feelings accompanied by serious thought and reflection. In an interesting study carried out in the early 1970's, a team of research specialists sought to find out some of the more important curative factors that came to play in the work of people involved in encounter groups. What they found, in summary, was that persons who concentrated *simply* on feelings did not make gains that were as positive or as lasting as those changes made by persons who *reflected* on what was happening to them before making decisions. That is a helpful confirmation of the process that I am suggesting to you. "Going off half cocked" is a poor way to help yourself over the long haul.

If you have been reading this book straight through, you may remember my talking about the power you have in your current situation that you did not have in the decision your parents made to divorce. Because of the maturity you have as a teen-ager or a young adult in the twenties, there is much more capacity and influence in you to affect the place or places that you now call home. If you are not married, that includes the homes in which you live with your parents. If you are married, it goes on to include the home that you share with your spouse. Of course, it involves the current place where you are living, regardless of who else is there. The point of all this is to say that you now, by your actions, can see to it that home is a place of unhappiness or that it functions well.

The next few chapters are my attempts to deal with some of the more common experiences in which you who are reading this book might find yourselves. Chapter 11 speaks to the teen-ager who still lives with a parent. There is no choice about that just now, but there are choices to be made about what that living condition will be like.

Following that, Chapter 12 deals with the situation of the older teen-ager or young adult who is not living with either parent on a regular basis. That chapter gets at the ambivalence that may go on about how involved you should or should not be in the life of those parents. It will talk about the experience of obligation to be at home during the rough times.

Then, Chapter 13 deals with the decision of whether counseling is needed and what to expect from it. Following that, I want to talk about legal factors and information that may be helpful to you.

11. Still Living at Home

If you are still in junior high or high school, you probably are living with one or the other of your parents. What that situation is like may vary a great deal. That makes it tough for me to begin to talk about things to do. It wouldn't be fair for me to make very specific suggestions. My plan, instead, is to speculate about the various kinds of things you are dealing with. We'll consider the possibilities that exist for you. Then, your responsibility is to decide—and do— something according to your plans. The place to start, though, is with your needs.

Faithfulness

One of the most important issues for *anyone* during the adolescent years is faithfulness. The word is so general that it may mean many things to you. Some other terms that may help to clarify it are dependability, consistency, trust, and durability. I guess what it boils down to is the question, "Whom can I count on?" That is a very important issue for you during the early teen-age years, and if it isn't settled very well, then it continues for many more years. Another question closely connected is, "What would it take for someone to leave me?" It's the same issue in the other direction. How much can you count on others? How much can they count on you?

Don't leave me yet. This is far more than a theoretical issue, and there is some important deciding that you have to do about it.

If your parents are divorced, you have had an experience in your life that deeply affects your own willingness to count on other people. There are two people, perhaps more significant to you than any others, who have promised to be counted upon by each other. And now they have chosen not to keep the promise, whatever the reasons. What you have learned from that, in a very powerful way, is that people don't always keep promises. You knew that already, of course, about minor promises. Now, however, you have seen it with one of the most important kinds of promises, Because of that you have to decide some things, and there are a good many choices before you.

One option is for you to decide not to take big promises very seriously. That goes two ways. You won't believe other people's promises, and you won't worry about making them yourself, because you can always change your mind later. That is a *decision* that you can make about your life. Without the divorce coming to pass, you might not have had to wrestle with that decision. You may not have thought about it even now. But your behavior, your actions, will begin to act on that principle many times out of your very deep hurt. That's the reason I have gone through the discussion of your feelings and your thoughts before now. My hope is that you will make decisions instead of just slipping into a kind of

behavior without considering the reasons and the consequences.

Let's follow this option a little further. If you decide to
take promises less seriously, that is also a decision to trust
people less. There are some gains and losses that come with
that. A gain is that you will be less likely to get hurt if you
don't count on people very much. It avoids the risk of being
disappointed. I remember one student telling me that he
never tried as hard as he could on a test. The reason? If he
did try that hard and did not make a good score, then he
would have to accept the fact that he wasn't as smart as he
thought. So he preferred never to try hard and then tell
himself that his low score only indicated that he had done
less than he was capable of doing.

That same kind of example goes on in relationships all the
time. Perhaps you remember a promise that a parent made
to take you to a movie when you were a child and then didn't
do it. The disappointment at not seeing the movie may have
been strong, but even stronger was that you had *counted on*
the parent and the parent had not kept the promise. Carry
that a step further to important relationships you might
form with friends. You may prefer to count on yourself
instead of on them for getting things done, for keeping
secrets, in order to keep from being disappointed.

The gain of not keeping promises is to avoid being hurt,
but there is also a loss. The loss is most evident in feeling
lonely. If you don't count on others, then you are not really
close to them. And the lack of closeness leads to loneliness.
Some sons and daughters of divorced parents have told me
of getting many phone calls from friends wanting to know
all about what happened. These calls often led to disappoint-

ment because the stories and confidences were then spread around school. What was needed, instead of a gossip, was a friend—someone who would listen and care and keep confidence. After such an experience, some of these people decided to talk to no one. And the result was often a sense of having to be on guard and thus being alone, when what they wanted was understanding and a place to talk.

The period after the divorce of parents is often a time when a friend becomes especially important. It may not even matter how old the friend is. You have to make a decision whether to trust your friend. In other words, will you count on your friend to be faithful to you?

The need for faithfulness, as I said earlier, is one that is shared by all people. You probably can think of folks who don't seem to care a whole lot about that. They depend on themselves and no one else. Many of them have gone through experiences much like yours. Somewhere along the line these experiences led them to the decision that independence was more important than the risk of getting hurt. I hope that you'll decide otherwise.

You certainly need some privacy during these years. And when something very hurtful has happened in your life, such as the divorce of your parents, you probably need even more. Those are times to brood, to think, or just to do nothing and listen to music or look out of the window. Important things happen during those times. A "repair operation" can be going on. *But* you also need to do some repairing or building of the new relationship you have with your parents.

Take the parent you're living with. You need some agreements about what faithfulness is in your new relationship.

It may mean the agreement that you have a right to your private time. It may also mean that, along with getting uninterrupted time, you become a faithful family member in dealing with problems in the home. Those problems can run all the way from deciding who takes out the garbage to being willing to listen for a while when someone is feeling down. You aren't *replacing* the parent who is no longer at home, but you will be assuming some of the functions that person provided before. The decision you face is *how* or in what manner you will do that. And the decision you make sets a tone for the way things will go in the household.

I don't want this to sound as though I'm laying a sermon on you to "be good." I do want to let you know that *you make a difference* in how things go. If you are still angry, you may tend to blame everything on the parent you are living with and see to it that things stay pretty miserable for the parent. "I'll show you" is the internal feeling. If the parent thinks it was bad before the divorce, you can make things a lot worse.

On the other hand, if your feeling is one of sadness and grief, you may tend to be more immobile, just not energetic enough to do much, leaving the work to the parent. Sooner or later that can lead to conflict as well, for which you are responsible partially. The decision to be faithful may mean forcing yourself to do things to make the household *work* even though you don't always *feel* like it! Your parent-at-home is struggling with those very same feelings, having to make a home work in spite of feelings of anger, depression, guilt, or whatever else. Some good, candid discussions of what that's like for both of you would probably be very helpful. That's part of what being faithful to each other means—hanging in there with each other during tough times.

SOMEBODY NEW IN THE HOUSE

There's another dimension that may come into play with your faithfulness, and it revolves around the remarriage of the parent-at-home. Suddenly there is somebody new in the house whom you don't know very well, but the person is in the role of a parent.

There will probably be some agreements about how that relationship is to be handled. You may not be ready to confide in that new person. After all, instant trust is not very likely in any relationship. And when this new person is moving into the spot formerly held by someone you loved, it can be rough. The more opportunity you had to get to know the person before the move, the better. But even then, some real adjustments have to be made. Usually, at first, your faithfulness to your real parent becomes the reason for you to be accepting of this new relationship, and it's important to admit that, at least to yourself.

Then come the tougher parts. I hope that you will feel free to confide in your parent about concerns you have and that the day will come when that can be done with your parent's new spouse. That doesn't always happen, I admit.

THE PARENT AWAY FROM HOME

Faithfulness includes the parent with whom you no longer live. What will that relationship be like? You will have a lot to do with that. It will be affected by where you are with your anger, sadness, etc. And you will have to make some decisions about how much that relationship means to you and whether it is worth putting up with the inconvenience of moving back and forth in order to get in visits with the other parent.

Part of your faithfulness to both of your parents will be to avoid getting into the position of carrying messages back and forth between them that simply help them to fight with each other. You can refuse to do that and say in plain terms that you don't intend to foster competition between them over you.

Some of the teen-agers who have helped me with this book have talked about the difficulties of spending time with both parents. If there is a lot of moving back and forth, you don't really have a consistent community of your own. Maintaining two sets of friends, two sets of clothes, two different living quarters, etc., gets to be pretty much of a hassle after a while. That's another spot at which you have to make a decision about what you need in order to be faithful to yourself. And maintaining deep friendships, staying regularly involved with social possibilities in your school, etc., may come to have precedence over taking off every weekend to visit your parent away from home. This is another aspect I hope you will sit down and talk over with them so that they understand what kinds of things *you need* in order to give yourself some stability in the midst of the instability. Of course, if both parents live close to each other, some of these kinds of problems can be relieved.

THIS AND THAT ABOUT FAITHFULNESS

There are all kinds of things that come about in this new situation in which you are finding yourself. And the possible complications could never be summarized in this book. One person talked briefly about the difficulty of deciding who gets to come to the high school graduation. After all, if both parents have remarried and there are numerous close friends and relatives and you get only ten invitations to distribute, who gets to come? How do you make sure that a happy occasion doesn't turn sour by having people together who don't want to be? All those events can tax your ingenuity and make you wonder about being faithful to anybody.

The most important thing I want to say to you about this whole issue is *to be faithful to yourself!* That doesn't mean you should be selfish, of course. It does mean that your parents' decision to divorce puts you in the position of taking more charge of how you will cooperate with both of them. They need your care, but so do you. They will want time from you, but you need time from you, too. They will want you to share in their new life, but you are having to build a new life for yourself as well as being a part of theirs. I think you can do both, cooperate with them and take care of yourself. But there may be times when you have to be pretty strong-willed about the whole thing.

Take time for yourself. Work to have friends that are consistent. Find resources, either in your parents or in someone else, to use when you need a place of privacy or a place to talk.

The most important issue of the teen-age years is the formation of who you are going to be. That includes decisions about your future, about the kinds of relationships you will have, about the vocation you will choose, and about the general style of life you want to experience. You can learn from what your parents have gone through, and I hope you will. Otherwise, you are a victim of it.

12. No Longer at Home

The preceding chapter dealt with the teen-ager who ordinarily still lives in the home of one of the parents. This chapter is concerned with you who are not living at home with either. You may be in college, finished with your schooling and now working and living away from your parents, or you may be married yourself. While there is no immediate daily contact, the divorce of parents still leaves you with decisions to make.

Some of these decisions revolve around the concept of faithfulness that I talked about in the previous chapter. These questions revolve around the contact you maintain with each parent, how much, how often, and whether you even want to have contact. One young man, about twenty-one years old, told me that after his parents divorced he broke off much contact with them. "They have gone their way," he said, "and I'm going mine." A young woman reported her unhappiness about being so neglected by her parents during their divorce that she would now neglect them in their recovery. Such is the response of many who don't have to be at home.

On the other hand, there are many who feel deeply responsible for bringing happiness and relief to the parental victims of divorce. They make frequent phone calls, visits every weekend, and even think it may be important to move back in with one or the other.

Those are the extreme choices that some make. Most of you probably wind up somewhere in between. Again, I can't make specific suggestions to you in a book. That would be to disregard the uniqueness of your situation. What I can do is remind you of some important factors going on in your life and theirs, hoping this will provide perspective.

The concept of faithfulness is still important for you. Some decisions have to be made about the nature of your relationship to your parents. Let's face it, however: you are away from them, and you and they are going to be making decisions that do not place children or parents as the first priority.

Your Parents

In the chapter on sadness, I described the grief process through which people move after suffering a loss. Your parents may be moving through that in very different ways. Some race into new relationships as a way of avoiding the pain of the separation. The result may be an array of partners or a quick marriage. With you away from home, there is even less pressure on them to "worry" about what effect their choices will have on you. It is hoped that is not the case to an extreme degree. Some information needs to be exchanged and introductions made, but your home is elsewhere now. And new relationships for your parents may give you a sense of relief about how much you need to worry about them.

Another possibility, however, is that one or both parents will settle into a more despairing kind of behavior. Isolation, staying home, dropping out of social activities, and either many or no phone calls indicate great difficulties. You may feel pressure, either from them or from yourself, to drop everything and move in to improve the situation.

Even further, one or both parents may pursue a very responsible and careful adjustment to the new reality in their lives. There may be a more patient search for a new mate and resulting happiness after a long period of time. Or there may be a long time of not finding someone else, accompanied by deeper and deeper pain. You can sense it from afar and grieve with them at their hurt.

The decision to remain single is, of course, another possibility. Fulfillment is found in other endeavors and there is no desire to repeat marriage, either out of fear of another failure or out of conviction that it is not as important as it once was.

These options and many more may all be seen by you from afar, and the options chosen by your parents may or may not agree with your hopes and dreams for them. But the reality is that, in your absence, your parents are making decisions over which you have a lessened influence, and it should be that way.

In a real sense, your divorced parents are having to deal with the developmental tasks of young adulthood all over again. The basic issue of the young adult years revolves around the choice of a mate or the choice not to enter into such a relationship. The word often used to describe this is intimacy. Does the person make a choice to enter into an intimate relationship, or is the choice to maintain distance? Distance can be maintained in many ways. A quick succession of partners is a distance-preserving life-style, because no one person is remained with long enough for any real caring and the accompanying vulnerability to develop. Isolation and avoidance of relationships is another way.

These are the same tasks that you are having to deal with in your young adult development, and seeing a parent or parents involved in the same thing can be both delightful and confusing. Care must be exercised not to imitate them unknowingly or to let their choices become automatic directions for you. That leads us to talking about you.

INTIMACY AND RISK

One young adult wrote that the divorce of his parents was his first realization of "insurmountableness." It was, he said, a "deathlike loss of the unit which was my life structure during growth." The question that followed that for him was whether another relationship could be better or clearer.

Questions such as that are not concerned simply with the relationship of one's parents. They are questions raised about one's own relationships. After all the "experiments" of adolescence with faithfulness, young adulthood is the time when you make a decision whether to enter into a more permanent relationship. If the experiences of your teen-age years have been successful, you have enough self-knowledge to know what you want and need in a mate. Or, you may come to the decision that there is no mate who will meet them.

Experiencing the divorce of your parents provides you with some unique excuses to use for whatever you choose. The failure of their marriage can become your rationale for not getting married. Or it can become the excuse to marry with such determination that nothing could break it up. Further, you could marry with a view that it may or may not work, resulting in putting a fairly small degree of emotional investment into it. Result? Probably a divorce of your own.

The level of involvement that you maintain with your parents can also become a strength or a liability in your own intimate relationships. Too much interference by your parents with their problems can test your own marriage, and limits may have to be set. Or, the lessons learned from their experience can strengthen your own marriage.

My point in all this is to be sure you are aware that being away from home doesn't do away with the influence that the divorce *can* have on your own marital experience or on the decision you make about whether to marry. That's the reason it is important to examine feelings, thoughts, and actions. Make sure you know some of the influences exerted here. Some examination of all this with a counselor can be helpful. Certainly, if you are intending to marry, it would be important to seek premarital counseling of some kind to examine your own relationship and how it may be affected.

Intimacy has been described in many ways. At base, I think it has to do with the willingness to trust another human being implicitly. It means believing that the other person will act with an interest in your welfare. It means believing that it is important to talk with each other about uncomfortable issues rather than avoiding them for fear that the relationship will be damaged seriously. It means being willing to take risks rather than trying to avoid changes taking place. It means having a commitment to the other that is based on more than feelings.

Such intimacy is possible only after you have gone through the difficult years of experimentation in adolescence. During those years, you get impressions about whether such intimacy is possible. You have to decide whether it is worth working for. The divorce of parents throws some new evidence into your considerations. Does their divorce mean that intimacy is not possible? Does it mean that the cost is too great? Or, does it mean that intimacy must be achieved in ways other than they pursued it? Can you learn from their mistakes?

In one way, no longer being at home gives you more freedom to wonder about all these things without the pressure. You can develop independent sources for information and thinking about your own life plan. I hope that as you do so, it will not be in isolation. There are many persons around who can be trusted and can be helpful. They can help you see things that you might have ignored or missed. You can make responsible decisions about how to be faithful to your parents and to learn from their mistakes. By doing so, you can find a way to intimacy that both gives and receives rather than feel compelled or trapped by what happened to them. Furthermore, if they have found more loving and intimate marriages since their divorce, you can rejoice with them rather than remain embittered by what happened in their lives earlier.

13. Is Counseling Needed?

It is obvious to you, I'm sure, that it is very important to me that you have plenty of understanding of the effects of divorce on you and your life. This entire book is written because of my belief in that. In fact, this book is one of a series of pastoral counseling aids which are to be used by pastors as additional helps for people who are going through a tough time in their lives or who are involved in a difficult decision-making process. Counseling may or may not be a part of that, but the authors of these various books believe that people need outside assistance to help them make realistic choices.

I don't believe that everyone whose parents go through a divorce *has* to have counseling. It would be silly to generalize like that. I do believe, however, that people cannot get as good an understanding of themselves in isolation as they can get in careful, responsible conversation with someone who cares about them. You may be able to get that kind of response from a close friend, a relative, or your parents. But sometimes it is very helpful to get it from someone who stands outside the whole situation. For that reason, I want to talk with you about what counseling is, what you can expect from it, and how you go about choosing someone.

WHAT IS COUNSELING FOR?

There are many descriptions of what counseling is for. Some people describe it as a process to get answers, and that is partly true. Others say that its purpose is to bring about change. That also is partly true.

For me, however, those descriptions are only some of the hopes that people bring to counseling. What it *is* is something far deeper than that. I like to describe it as "relational" in nature. That is, it is intended to provide you with a relationship. Well, you may say, I've got plenty of those already. But this is a particular *kind* of relationship. It is one that is *intended* to be faithful and trustworthy from the very first, even if you have doubts about whether that is even possible or not.

When you think of counseling, ordinarily it is because you have problems. The problems are usually connected with a relationship. People go for counseling after a death, when they have lost a relationship. They go for counseling when a marriage is in trouble, a relationship going poorly. Parents or children seek counseling when things are not going well between them. The list can go on and on.

Counseling, in my understanding, is intended to provide you with a relationship within which you can work out how to handle your other relationships. Since a divorce is a marriage gone bad that will affect in some way your view of marriage for yourself, it is a relationship problem for you. And you *need* to have a tie, a bond with someone to assist you in understanding what happened and to help you *learn* from what went wrong so that you run less risk of repeating it. Also, if handled properly, the counseling relationship itself helps you to experience a healthy relationship and to learn how to maintain one. We all need that, whether we get it from a professional counselor or someone else.

The church that I served in Louisville, Kentucky, was deeply affected by a tornado in the spring of 1974. The homes of many of our members were completely destroyed. For ten days after that, the church became a huge feeding center. People came there regularly every day to eat, not because they couldn't afford to eat elsewhere. They had been through a real crisis, they were tired, and they needed to talk about what had happened to them. Families had told each other over and over what had gone on during and after the storm, and that wasn't enough. They began to need to tell their stories to someone else. Their relationships weren't cracking, by any means, but they needed more support. Other people sitting around those tables became the "someone else" that each person needed. You could watch the people sitting around each day, finding someone else to tell their story to, and listening to the stories of the ones who had first listened to their stories.

That is the role that a counselor plays. He or she is the "someone else" during hard times. That is the relationship to which you can go to tell your story and to examine it and to learn from it. Those people sitting around the tables with each other at the church were effective counselors for each other. It was a dramatic situation, though. Unusual. Unfortunately, divorce is not that unusual, and therefore people are not always willing to listen. They are dealing with other concerns. You, however, if affected deeply, need someone to listen to help you over the critical period and to help you make decisions in the aftermath.

As one young adult wrote to me: "Divorce is fairly common now, almost fashionable, and it's assumed that kids just adapt. . . . But their ideas are still in the formulating stages and often they don't know that the splitting . . . is quite traumatic. I hope that kids understand that it's O.K. to be upset about The Divorce. I had felt that it was such a run-of-the-mill thing that it was stupid to be sad." She says very well what could be the case for you if you don't find listening ears. You'll clam up, think you shouldn't be upset, and in the process lose out in terms of your own development.

That's what counseling's for—to help you keep growing by having a relationship that provides health as you struggle with the pains of a relationship that went bad.

What Do You Expect in Counseling?

Many jokes are around about what counseling is like. Some of them make fun of what is called nondirective methods. You've heard them. The patient sits down and says, "I feel awful today." The doctor nods sagely and responds, "You're feeling badly." My colleague in teaching calls that the "old fool" response. The intent is to show understanding, but what it does instead is sound mechanical and artificial. Other caricatures come from impressions of sensitivity groups and describe various "exercises" to teach you how to trust, such as walking blindfolded with someone else leading you through a large room.

Such jokes have enough realism about them to make us wary. I want to describe to you briefly what you should expect from good counseling. The first thing you should expect is that it will take a while for you to feel comfortable. Anytime you walk into a room and are expected to talk about things that really matter, it is awkward for you. You want to know whether you can trust this person. So, for several sessions, you and the counselor must get to know each other if you haven't met already. You can expect to talk a good deal about yourself and your history, the things you have been through that have meant a lot to you. This provides the counselor with some understanding about *you,* because you are the one who is important here.

Second, you can expect the counselor to do a lot of listening. You may at first think that he or she is going to do no more than that. Perhaps all the jokes about nondirective counseling seem to be coming true. But for a counselor to start telling you things to do or making judgments about other people right away would be a sign to be wary of. Quick advice and instant solutions may be a sign that you are not being taken seriously and that someone is just throwing around pat answers that may not fit your situation. The important point in this is whether you feel that the person is *really* listening to you or is just playing a role. You can get an impression pretty quickly about that. A good counselor won't just repeat your words back. She or he will say things in different ways to make sure you have been understood. You may be asked to think about things from a different perspective in order to help you understand all that has gone on in different ways. Enjoy being listened to. I'll bet it doesn't happen very often.

Third, you should expect a good counselor eventually to begin to push you. That doesn't mean anything violent, of course. It does mean that some of your interpretations may be questioned. If your behavior doesn't fit with what is happening, the counselor should wonder out loud about that. This relationship is going to be honest. If things don't make sense, you both should be willing to say so. Feelings become easier to talk about, because the relationship is a candid one. Uncomfortable things can be voiced without fear of the relationship collapsing. In that kind of relationship you can feel more freedom to understand yourself and the people who are most important to you. That may even mean that you and the counselor get mad or disappointed with each other from time to time, but the bond continues. It becomes a place where difficulties are faced rather than avoided.

WHY SHOULD I GET COUNSELING?

As I've said earlier, I don't believe that everyone needs professional counseling. You may have a friendship with someone that provides all those characteristics I've just talked about. If you do, I'm happy for you. If you don't, that may be as good a reason as any to seek out professional counseling.

Getting counseling doesn't mean you're "crazy" or out of control. It simply means that you need a relationship for a time to help you deal with some areas that concern you.

Of course, there may be more serious reasons as well. For instance, if you find that you are staying angry most of the time and taking it out on everybody in general, I think it is important for you to talk that out with someone who has the training to be helpful to you. The same goes for depression or deep sadness that seems to envelop you and leave you unable or unwilling to involve yourself with other people. Perhaps you are finding yourself confused a good deal of the time. All of those are signals indicating that you *ought* to seek out some help. Things are really getting to you.

Whether those most serious signals are going on, or whether you would just like to sit down with someone for that one purpose of figuring things out, give some consideration to it. It could be a very helpful experience.

Whom Should I Go To?

The lists of counselors are very long. There are all types. Psychiatrists, clinical psychologists, social workers, marriage and family counselors, pastoral counselors, and parish ministers are the most common people who have formal training. This book, of course, is written with the primary notion that you may have already consulted a minister in some way. Often, ministers are more known to you if you are connected with a church. If your interests are too demanding of them, they know responsible people to whom they can refer you. Often, however, a parish minister can provide you with an informal but faithful context in which you can talk about yourself and your concerns.

In making your choice, however, consider some other important aspects. One is that you are *comfortable* in talking with this person. That may not be true in the first conversation or two, but if you don't begin to trust her or him, then you should say so and ask to see someone else. If you don't get over the discomfort, you won't get as much out of it. And there are some relationships that just don't work out, regardless of how much both people want it to. So, don't think you have to stay just because the person is professional. It is the *relationship* that is just as important.

14. Some Legal Factors

It occurred to me that it would be helpful for you to know some of the legal procedures and issues that take place in a divorce. Legal terms are used a lot, and you may have heard them but do not understand what they mean. Please bear in mind that I am not a lawyer, and any specific information you need should be obtained from such a professional. But there are some general descriptions that may be helpful to you. Of course, even these vary from state to state.

GROUNDS

States vary on whether "grounds" must be established in order for a divorce to proceed or whether two persons may divorce by common agreement. In states where blame must be fixed or some sort of reason established, a divorce can become even more painful than it would be anyway. For instance, one partner may have to accuse and prove the other partner guilty of desertion, cruelty, adultery, sodomy, conviction of a felony, or any one of various other "grounds." To prove this, the word of the accusing partner is not enough. There usually must be some sort of proof in the form of other witnesses or circumstantial evidence. If you will remember the stages of deterioration that I discussed in the chapter on "Accept What Happened," you will see how this process of accusation can lend itself to more difficulties. You may have heard such accusations thrown around between your parents in the process of divorcing. If so, you can't help wondering which came first, the decision to divorce or the "reason." They may have found the reason afterward instead of before, in order to meet the requirements of the law.

Some states now provide what is commonly called "No Fault" divorce. Such laws do not require the partners to establish any "guilt" or misconduct on the part of either. The partners may simply declare the marriage no longer acceptable to them. The laws may require a certain period of time to pass between the filing of the request for divorce and the actual granting of it. Many people, myself included, feel that this procedure makes much more sense because it makes it more difficult for the partners to use the law as a way of clubbing each other.

Support

Another difficult issue following a divorce is the division of property and the agreement as to whether continuing financial support will be provided by one for the other. Disputes often arise over what is "fair" and courts often must rule on the settlement.

As you can well imagine, if one person being proven "guilty" of something means that the person must "pay" the other partner because of it, great court fights can take place between two persons trying to prove each other guilty of various kinds of misconduct. That's another reason, for me, that the "No Fault" divorces are more humane. In those cases, agreements about support are based more on need than on guilt. For instance, if the wife has not worked outside the home during the marriage, then the court may direct the husband to provide support and/or education for her for a reasonable time to help her become more independent. This kind of arrangement makes far more sense. It bases the decisions on need rather than on punishment.

There are two different kinds of support to have in mind here. One is direct support to one spouse or the other. In various states it may be referred to as alimony, maintenance, spousal support, etc. Whatever the name, it is money provided directly to an ex-partner to be used as the person sees fit.

A second form is called child support. There are more restrictions on its use, for your benefit. It is money provided by the partner not living in the home to the one living there to be used specifically for the care of the child or children. This can be for food, clothing, medical and dental needs, and for education. Other specific uses may be stated. There is no set scale for the amount of money, and courts vary on how much they expect the partner to give. The amount is usually based on the financial ability of the parents at the time of the divorce and may be adjusted in later years according to changing circumstances.

This is another spot at which conflict may occur. Even though the support is for the children of the marriage, some partners will use it as a means for threatening the other. "If you don't quit bothering me, I'll take you to court for more

child support!" When this happens, it takes some real perspective for you to understand that the issue is their conflict
and not some disagreement about how much you are really
worth.

CUSTODY

Who "gets" the children? Here is where much of the pain
occurs in its deepest form. When two persons choose to
dissolve their marriage, that does not mean they want to
dissolve their relationship with their children. Yet, one must
to some degree, in the form of no longer living with them
regularly. This is another spot at which battles may take
place. Even in states where "No Fault" is the rule in terms
of the divorce, some parents have used the issue of child
custody to get at each other by trying to prove that the other
is "unfit" to be a parent.

The aim of courts is to grant custody to the parent most
able to "care for, control, and direct" the child. Thus, the
provision of child support is often for the purpose of allow-
ing the parent with custody to spend more time with the
child. This is considered more important with younger children, ordinarily.

With older children, like yourself, the court often asks the
preference you have. Making a choice can be a very difficult
moment for you and needs to be talked about a bit later.
Hearings often take place in a lawyer's office or before a
commissioner or judge to work out these arrangements.

Some states now allow parents to have joint custody of the
children, rather than one or the other having to gain custody. It is assumed in such cases that the parents can negoti-

ate with each other about the place for the child to live. It also allows for changes to be made without going through court procedures each time. Even more important, it doesn't put the child in the position of "belonging" to one parent or the other.

BENEFITS

I am not as familiar with other benefits available to you as I would like to be, but I know there are some worth checking into. For instance, Social Security sometimes makes provision for education and other support of children in the case of divorce. There are also some benefits available to the children of veterans. The benefits from these various sources are worth checking into for your particular situation.

WHERE DO YOU COME IN?

These comments provide you with some basic information that I think is important for you to know. The older you are, the more input you have in what happens. You really do have some power and influence in what happens to your parents and to you.

In the best of circumstances, if you are still a minor, you can sit down with your parents as they work out their agreements and talk about your preferences. What kind of education would you like them to provide for you? Where would you prefer to live? You may identify concerns that they may not have thought of.

In the worse situations, you may let them know loudly and clearly that you do not appreciate being used as a means for them to hurt each other. Don't panic and get caught up in the battles. Tell them your hurt and your anger about sacrificing your welfare for the sake of having more ammunition to use on each other.

In either case, it is wise to sit down and think about your future. What do you need in terms of support? That may mean education. It may mean getting counseling, and if you go to professionals, that can cost money, which you should ask them to provide. You need a constant community to live in without having to shuffle back and forth too much, and you should work on ways to have that for yourself. If they are going to be living a good distance apart, what kinds of visitation would you like to have? They need to hear from you, but in the emotion of the moment they may not think to ask.

Of course, if you are away from home, there is less opportunity and necessity for you to be involved in this. But it is still worth asking about if your education is still to be completed, health needs to be cared for, etc. Also, you can provide some perspective because of your distance.

P.S.

I wrote this book for a lot of reasons. The most important ones center around my belief that the sons and daughters of divorce often get neglected in the whole process. The result is a real feeling of your being "left."

I believe that you need time and space to understand the divorce and its impact on you. That understanding can help you to survive without scars that forever contaminate your own views and hopes for close relationships.

I believe that you need a community to support you. That's true all the time but especially during this time. My being a minister means that a church community comes to mind, but I know that churches are made up of people. Some people understand and are sensitive, and some don't. I hope you will reach out to some community, whether it is a church, a special group of friends, or some other organization. Whichever it is, they should be a group who will do more than comfort you. They should help you to grow.

It's hard for a book like this to seem very personal. But as I have written it, I have tried to think about sons and daughters of divorced parents whom I know. I hope that has made it seem more personal for you.

You are a real person of worth, a child of God. That means there are a lot of resources in you. It means that there are a lot of others around who can help. Use them. It will be good for you and good for them, too.

For Further Reading

Arnold, William V., et al. *Divorce: Prevention or Survival.* Westminster Press, 1977.

Several years ago, a group of divorced persons met with me in a church for many sessions to discuss the issues involved. The result was this book, which would be informative for your understanding of the factors that lead to divorce, as well as issues that divorced persons must face. It would be helpful for your further understanding of what has taken place.

Gardner, Richard A. *The Boys and Girls Book About Divorce.* Bantam Books, 1971.

This book was written by Dr. Gardner for younger children in elementary school. However, many adults and older children of divorced parents have found it very helpful. He discusses the feelings children of divorce often experience and provides helpful understanding to get you through the tough spots.

Richards, Arlene, and Willis, Irene. *How to Get It Together When Your Parents Are Coming Apart.* David McKay Co., 1976.

This book has a similar interest to the one you have just read. The authors discuss marriage problems, feelings children have during the divorce and after the divorce. It concludes with a guide to getting help. If reading has been helpful to you already, this would be a good continuation.

Satir, Virginia. *Peoplemaking.* Science and Behavior Books, Inc., 1972.

This is a delightful book which provides a great deal of understanding of communication patterns in families. In addition, Mrs. Satir makes many suggestions about improvement of communication and understanding of family dynamics. It is both informative and enjoyable.